LETTERS TO
My Lady
My Best Friend
My Wife

REV. LEROY WRIGHT JR.

authorHOUSE®

AuthorHouse™
1663 Liberty Drive
Bloomington, IN 47403
www.authorhouse.com
Phone: 1 (800) 839-8640

Published by AuthorHouse 09/04/2015

ISBN: 978-1-5049-4715-2 (sc)
ISBN: 978-1-5049-4714-5 (e)

Print information available on the last page.

This book is printed on acid-free paper.

KJV
Scripture quotations marked KJV are from the Holy Bible, King James
Version (Authorized Version). First published in 1611. Quoted from the KJV
Classic Reference Bible, Copyright © 1983 by The Zondervan Corporation.

Contents

Her Response

I have prayed and searched for a long time, looking for someone who could understand me and what I wanted out of life. I have mistakenly married the wrong women, erroneously thinking God was leading me in those decisions. Some of them were a hindrance in the goals I had set for my life. They tried to influence me to go in a different direction than where God was leading me. I could not do that because I fear and respect God. I could not overlook my duty as head of the household. That is why I have stood and always will stand for righteousness in the eyes of God. Later, I found myself praying asking God for a home of peace and He has blessed me with that. Therefore, I am writing this book, dedicating it to the woman who I have met and found her to know more about me than some in my past who only thought they knew me. We think alike and we both want the same things out of life. The more we talked, the more we realized that we understood each other to the point that we could almost say, we were raised in the same household. I truly thank her parents for bringing her up to have self-respect and respect for others. That is an "A-plus" in my eyes. I truly thank God for leading me to meet the person who has some of the same characteristics that I have. I thank Him for giving me the opportunity to express the way I feel. It is a joy to be able to express myself to someone who knows when the hand of God is leading her to someone set aside just for her. I also thank her for understanding that I am looking forward to treating her like the queen she is. Yes, there are some differences and we are both mature enough to sit and talk about any issues and come to an agreement that pleases us both. Therefore, to Clara Wright, the love of my life, "Thank you, baby, for understanding and loving me for who I am and giving me the chance to love you the same way. I consider it a blessing and an honor to have this chance to respect, love and cherish you like the beautiful woman that you are. You are a very special woman who sees the love in me that has been put there by God. I am also a blessed man to see the love of God in you."

To Clara

Thank you for allowing me to open my heart and tell you what I was feeling. You received it with a positive attitude, which caused me to express myself even more. Now, I can treat you like the queen that you are, something I was not allowed to do in my past relationships. Others from my past received this type of sharing with negative attitudes. You gave me the chance to show and tell you what was going through my mind. Thank you for letting me become the willing king in your life and you, the willing queen in mine. In this book are poems and letters I wrote to you which express my love for you. Now, I can truly say I have found my soulmate. I really thank you for seeing the real me. It has always been my desire to love my wife and treat her like a queen. Sweetheart, I try to speak out of love bringing words that would capture your heart. I attempted, in the past, to express my deepest feelings of love to others but they fell on deaf ears which caused me to withdraw. Thank you for receiving me with an open heart and mind, allowing me to share my love with you that others were too blind to receive. Sweetheart, you shocked me when you said you want to thank the ones from my past who chose not to remain in my life. Only one other time, in my life, was I given a chance to share these feelings and that was with Carol. She encouraged me to express my inner feelings and has now gone home to be with the Lord. I thought I probably would never find another to share my deepest feelings with again but I was wrong because I have found that chance with you. Thank you for having respect for my memories of her who I loved and lost to death.

rust

If I can trust you with the words that come from my lips, then I can trust you with my love. If I can trust you with my love, then I can trust you with my heart. If I can trust you with my heart, then I can trust you with my life. If I can trust you with my life, then I can trust you in my home. If I can trust you in my home, then I know what goes on in my home will remain between you and me. If I can trust you with all of that, then I know I have found a true friend, a true love and a wife for life. Now, I can truly say you are all of this and more to me.

You Are My Reason

You, my love, are the reason I feel so blessed. I feel so connected that I can stand straight and tall. I feel like a tree which has leaves that stay green all the year round. I am the tree and you are my leaves. I can supply all you need to maintain your color from season to season from my connection to the earth. You cover my branches to keep me warm from the winter snow. You cast your shadow to protect my roots from the summer heat. In spite of all that you do for me, you still find time to share your love and to be shade for those who sit under us. Even for the birds, you become their resting place. I love you just the way you are. Do not ever change because I love the way you melt my heart.

Hook In My Heart

Why do I love you? Let me tell you. You caught my attention and you held it captive. You stopped my search and brought my wandering to an end. You opened my heart and walked right in with a smile that I could never forget. You spoke words so softly that caused me to stop in my tracks. I became blind to all others after seeing the beauty of your face. You opened your heart and with your love, you caused me to stay. You touched me in a way that others never knew how to. You said, "I love you," in a way that put a hook in my heart and you became the bait that I will never release. As I stared into your eyes, you leaned toward me and with your lips, you sealed it all with a kiss. Thank you, my lady, for being the one I have been looking for all of my life. I will hold you forever in my heart, my love. I will shower you with happiness because you filled the void that others could not. I will love you, my rose, with all of my heart until the end of time.

Waiting For Her

While sitting home waiting for my love to come walking through the door, my anticipation grew greatly. When she walked through the door, my eyes became wide open and from her beauty, my heartbeat began to race. Her hands were full and her head was covered. I closed the door behind her and helped with her things. When all was clear and her hands were free, she turned her attention toward me. I held her with tender love and gave her a kiss, one that I was hoping would never end. I could feel the warmth of her body next to mine. She had a look of such peace because she knew she was safe at home in my arms. Out of my mouth flowed these words of affection, "I love you babe because you are my queen."

Overwhelmingly Pleased

You leave me breathless as my love for you overflows. I extended my love to you with total trust. My heart is full and my mind is made up. I am overwhelmingly pleased with you, lady of my life. Do not ever change because it is very hard to find someone like you. I have been trying to find someone who understands me in a small way, but you have surely surpassed even that. In the near future, God will bring us together and there is but one thing that will separate us, that will be the will of God by death. You have been more of a wife to me than you will ever know. Thank you, my dear, for being my best friend, my wife.

Me In You

Good morning my love. Oh, how wonderful it is just to be alive to say, "Thank you Lord for my wife." What a blessing He has given to me. I know there is a beautiful lady on the other end of this message. She is my future, my best friend, my lovely queen and one who is worth tipping my hat to. She is also worth saving my love for, and one who He has been preparing and shaping to receive a love like mine. I have given praise to God with my whole heart and that love has overflowed onto you. How can I hurt me? How can I turn me down? How can I not love me? I love you because I see me in you. We agree on the important things in life on so many different levels and that makes me love you even more. I truly appreciate and open my arms to you, my best friend, my love, my rose and my queen.

A Tulip In A Pot

There was a single red flower sitting on the side of the road. It was standing tall with two green leaves. I began to notice that when traffic passed by, the rush of wind from the vehicles would cause it to bend over. After the wind receded, it would stand back up. One day, as I passed by, I noticed the plant was a single red tulip sitting in a pot. Someone in a hurry left it sitting in a pot on the side of the road and that is why it bowed every time someone passed by. They were too busy to notice the beauty of a single red flower sitting in a pot and they may have thought it was just growing wild. They may have been going too fast to see its beauty as it bowed trying to get their attention. Therefore, I picked up the pot and poured water on its roots. The leaves began to spread and shine as the healing water rejuvenated her roots. Today, this single red tulip has brought such joy into my life. I really thank all those who passed her by, for not only was she beautiful on the outside, but inwardly also. Today, she is a very special flower and here she sits, right by my side. She is the lady who has brought such joy into my life. I truly love her.

Voices From The Kitchen

As the winter rolled in, my wife, my honey, said she was cold. She crawled in next to me as I lay there in bed. I reached for and covered us with a warm blanket as she laid there in my arms, when I heard voices from the kitchen crying out, "What about us?" The sugar in the sugar jar was crying out, "We are sweet too." I cried out to the sugar, "But not as sweet as my honey who is lying here next to me." Then there was the milk crying out, "You need me for your coffee." I said to the milk, "I've already kissed my wife's breast and sipped from my cup. Now, the coffee in my cup is already golden brown just like her skin."

Missing Him

As she lay across her bed, waiting to hear from her love, she dreamed of him lying next to her. She took the pillow, where he had laid his head, and took a deep breath to smell the scent of his cologne. She held the pillow tight as her heart filled with love. When her phone rang out, she rushed to see if it was her love, to whom she could not wait to say, "Oh baby, how I've missed you."

Wonderful Woman

Good morning my love; God has done it again. Thank you Lord for my lovely lady, my best friend and soulmate. She is the most wonderful woman in the world, which you have set aside just for me. Thank you for preparing us for one another and bringing us together after many trials and tribulations. Thank you for my beautiful rose.

A Rose Just For Me

Now, for the beautiful flower that a single rose petal fell from in order to become a single red rose just for me, "Thank you, mother-in-law. You prepared and trained my rose to understand things that some people search for and never find in a lifetime, common sense and the ability to understand that which is being explained, something I did not observe in others whose paths I crossed. You have reared someone who knows and thinks the same way I do about life. She knows me better in a short period of time than others who previously spent years with me. They never really knew my character and were forever trying to change me to fit their lifestyle. Thank you for the beautiful rose who sprang from you."

My Wish

To the rose that shines in my life unconditionally, in the midst of rain, cloudy days, hazy days or sunshine, "Good morning darling, how are you? As I lie here with you on my mind, I am wishing I could be there to stroke your hair, kiss your neck, massage your shoulders and run my fingers down your spine. I would massage you with baby oil down to the tip of your toes, help you with your stockings and anything else that you need me to do. I love you baby. You are the sunshine in my rain, the glow in my smile and the pep in my step. Darling, you have me swinging on ropes bringing buckets of love to keep you glowing so everyone can see the gorgeous rose that God has prepared for me.

Biggest Inspiration

Hello, my dear; this is for you. I want you to know that all I want to do is love and please you. Besides God, you are my biggest inspiration. You are the reason I walk around with a smile on my face and joy in my heart. I am in love with you because you have given me a reason to look forward to life again. You have filled my days with gladness and uplifted a downtrodden soul. I salute you for being my biggest inspiration as we began our life together.

A Rose Out of Place

In my vision, I was walking and to my surprise, I came across a large field of beautiful, blue green grass. Above the grass there stood large, purple, tulip flowers. There was one that caught my attention. It seemed out of place it was different and it stood above all the rest. There it stood all alone, the most wonderful and beautiful red rose which reminded me of you. All the rest became invisible because I had finally found the one I had been looking for all my life, YOU! Therefore, I made my way over and laid next to you, my rose, to watch you dance back and forth as the wind blew. After lying there for awhile, I had to leave but before I did, I gave you a kiss to let you know I will be back to see you again.

Sugar And Spice

While sitting here looking at a picture of my lady, I began to think of her beauty. She is the lady who has my heart because she shows me how sweet she really is. I called her name in a loving way and she answered me back with the response, "Yes, baby." I cannot help but think she gives new meaning to sugar and spice. In all that she does for me, she always knows how to touch my heart.

Open Arms

The clouds became lonely in the quiet stillness of the night. They felt so alone that they began to cry. As their tears started toward the earth, the grass began to stand tall with outstretched arms singing, "Shower your love down on us." The wind began to blow and the trees began to bow and thank God. Here I lie thinking of ways to cover you with a heart full of love. Just like the grass, I welcome you warmly with open arms to tell you that I thank God for another chance to be in love with someone who is willing to love me back. Thank you, baby, because you have made life for me worth living again. You have helped bring the sunshine back into my world. Thank you for the radiant smile on my face and the joy which overflows in my heart.

Thank God

I find myself thanking God for you on this cold, clear morning. I thank Him for bringing us together. I also thank Him for the people He used in our lives to speak to us and turn us toward one another. Who would have ever known I would be saying that I am crazy about you at this point in our relationship. You stay on my mind and in my heart constantly causing me to become blind to all other women. My heart, mind and thoughts of you are enough to keep me waiting for you. Darling, when I said, "I love you and only you," I meant every word. There is no one else I would rather spend my time with than you. I love you, girlfriend. I love you my rose, who I met on the way to depression. Thank you for rescuing me.

Green Tender Plant

Good morning, again, my lady; how are you? As I think about you, I picture you as a fresh, green, tender plant just starting to spread your leaves. You are so tender, fresh and innocent just waiting for the sun to shine so you can stand tall. You are looking for me to come by to see you, to say that you are the reason I am here. I will watch over and protect you. I will support you and provide all the love you will ever need while helping you stand tall. My entire source comes from God and I share it with only you.

Most Beautiful Of Them All

I am a single, green stem on a large rose bush. There are many red roses but none as lovely as mine. Bees come by to leave their honey and butterflies fly by just to see her beauty. Ants climb up to steal her honey, but without success. A hummingbird comes by and flaps its wings, sending a cool breeze in the heat of the day. A lady stopped by to see my rose, and the words from her lips rang out, "The stem is so green and its rose is so bright. Of all the roses on this bush, this is the most beautiful one of them all."

Rose On My Arm

The rose on my arm was shining so bright with her gorgeous, red dress fitting just right. Heads are starting to turn as we walk through the room. Men are looking and women are talking. My head is held high and my chest is stuck out because I know that my lady is the queen of the night. We reached our table to take our seats, when the entertainer at the microphone forgot his speech. To our surprise, he spoke from his heart, "Oh my goodness, she is a beautiful sight." All the people began to clap as she rose from her seat and took a bow.

Something Has Gone Wrong

I heard that something had gone wrong because someone did not respect or fear God. Some are lonely and some are sad. The butterflies are confused and flying into one another and the bees have gone on an attack. The hummingbirds do not know which direction to fly, all because they cannot find my queen. She has slipped out of their sight but she had been there for them all of their lives. She had gone inside to look for her own love. She is now ready to start a life of her own with me so she can shine as she walks right by my side.

The Rose And The Butterfly

Well, good morning to my most beautiful rose and butterfly. I see you two have finally come together. Your colors are lovely and have really made it worth the wait. The hummingbird would have been here as well if she had known our paths would cross. However, since she is not present, I will take a picture to prove to her that you and the butterfly are not twins. I know the butterfly has somewhere to go because her wings continually flow. Nevertheless, before she leaves, I know one thing; she will kiss my rose to keep her from crying.

Winter Beauty

Winter has crept in to turn tree leaves brown but you, my dear, are still tall and green. Your leaves may droop and your limbs may bend from the weight of winter's snow but I know you will never grow weary. Birds still need you and so do I. I cannot wait to see you, just to sit and admire your winter beauty. Other trees are bare of their protective cover but you, my sweet, are covered and protected by my love.

God's Order

Good morning, my love. I arise on this cold winter morning to find the moon is still on its post. The sky is clear and the wind is cold. The stars are still twinkling because they all agree that the sun is coming to warm our day. It is shining so bright, we will not need any light. The sun has been ordered by God to brighten our day. Two lovers separated by distance can now find their way to become as one. Oh, how we have overcome all from the light that God has planted within us. Now, we stand on the mountaintop shouting, "Thank you, Lord, for bringing us together."

Same Umbrella

Only two noticed her in the past. They did not know how to cherish her or where to search for her true beauty. They did not see it because she kept it hidden, as one hides a diamond in the dark. I watched her, one day, as she came walking in my direction. The frozen smile on her face sent a signal saying, "No way." Her signal said, "No way" but my heart said to me, "Yes way." I told myself that one day she would surely be mine, when the time was right. Later, I spoke to her and she spoke back. This gave me a chance to open my heart to her. When she saw that, my intentions were pure she opened her heart to me and, now, we are under the same umbrella. I asked her out to a place of her choice, a place of good taste for a bite to eat. To my surprise, she knew of a place where suits and ties were required. It was a romantic place but some thought the prices were a bit too high. After we were seated, she went to the ladies' room and when she returned, the show was just beginning. She walked through the door wearing her beautiful, black, satin dress with a red rose in her hair. The red rose was saying, "I am proud to be here being shown off by this beautiful lady. The smile on her face makes me feel so good to be a part of my queen's date." The rose petals were unique because each stood on its own. The gorgeous black, satin dress was hugging her curves as she made her way across the room. It was making the statement, "I'm so proud to be worn by this queen. She has a beautiful smile on her face and is wearing me with such pride." The server followed her to see where she was sitting. When he saw me, he nodded as if to say, "You are a blessed man." I responded by lifting my hand to say, "I already know." People were taking pictures of her to show their friends her beautiful dress. They knew she was the queen of the night. We finished dinner but the night was still young, so I wanted to take her to a place of my choosing. I looked at my lady and said, "Now it is my turn." I took her to a place called Bowtie Required. This establishment was built only for kings with their queens. I removed my necktie, put on my bowtie and escorted my lady inside. When we walked through the door, kings and queens were already dancing. They all stopped when we entered the room. All the ladies stopped to see her beautiful, black, satin dress. The music was playing softly and slowly as I danced with my queen. To our surprise, we realized everyone had left the dance floor to watch as we danced. They all wanted to see her as she moved in her gorgeous, black, satin dress with the red rose in her hair. The rays from the light were shining just right, causing her skin to glow even more. The song stopped playing and the dance ended. Everyone began to clap as I took a bow on one knee to show my queen respectful thanks. After the dance was over and we started to leave, ones from her past were now seeing my queen's true beauty for the very first time. The smile on her face and the glow of her skin caught the attention of those who, at one time, had passed her by. Their mouths fell open, as they stared in disbelief realizing, in that moment, what a mistake they had made. Now that they have seen her, and their hearts have changed, it is too late because my queen has made her choice. Her heart is right; her head is held high and she knows I will always be by her side. She raised her hand to wave back at them, then turned to looked at me with those beautiful, brown eyes. Later, as she sat on the seat beside me in the car, with a contented smile on her face, she was unaware that her surprise was not over. We arrived home to find the news media there. Word had spread that a true queen was in town and they wanted to see her in that beautiful, black, satin dress with the red rose in her hair. One of them asked her, "What makes you happy? What does it take to keep the smile on your face?" She looked deeply into my eyes and, with pride, spoke these words, "There stands my tall drink of water; the man in my life who said I give new meaning to sugar and spice. There stands the man to whom I pledge all of my heart, all of my thoughts and all of my love. He keeps me warm, makes me smile and laugh, and knows what I need before I ask. With a love like his, I need no other. He always gives me unconditional love and trust. I thank others who did not see this man's heart and who let him go; my, what a blessing it has been for me." After speaking with the media, we went inside and to her surprise, pink and red rose petals led to the bedroom. I wanted her to know that I will always love her. There on the bed, I had placed a crown covered with diamonds and a matching necklace. I looked into her eyes as they filled with tears. She reached out, hugging me tightly, and whispered, "My king, whom I will always love, we will forever be under the same umbrella."

Because

Because I could not see you, I wondered, "Why?" Because I could not see you, my thoughts began to run wild. Because I could not see you, my body trembled with worry. Then, there was the sound of the door opening which caused me to arise. The wider it opened, the wider open my eyes became. As I eagerly awaited her entrance, in walked my sweetheart with a radiant smile greater than a breath of fresh air. My blood began to flow swifter than the mightiest river; my heart was pumping stronger than the wildest storm. My legs began to tremble so much that I could not stand; my feet wanted to run to her. She looked at me with those beautiful eyes, as she moved towards me whispering, "I love you." That is when I realized, I was standing there melting like sweet honey from the world's most popular bee. My queen smiled and professed her true love for me, as I held her like never before.

With Each Beat Of Her Heart

As I was walking through the room, passing by my sweetheart, I reached out and caught her by the hand. She paused as I stepped forward, pulling her soft body next to mine. The warmth of her body radiated with intense heat as she laid her head on my chest. I could feel the beating of her heart in prefect rhythm with mine. She lifted her face to mine; her pulse began to quicken with each beat, as we stared lovingly into each other's eyes. During that time of passion, we realized just how strong our love was.

Something Special About Her

People riding on a ferry began to watch the dolphins as they swam just off the bow. They watched and clapped as the dolphins jumped and spun with such force. The dolphins began to put on a special show until the people stopped watching them and turned their attention to another matter. They wondered why they were no longer the star of the show. My lady stepped out and made her way to that side of the ferry where the playful dolphins had been entertaining the throng of people. She looked over the rail at the dolphins who had ceased their playing. Now, they knew why the people's attention was no longer on them. They, too, now saw the beautiful woman who had stolen the attention of the people. Sinking down under the water, they all came up in an even row, standing on their tails in the water, clapping with their fins. After seeing my lady who was now the star of the show, the dolphins put on a special dance just for her as she stood watching them. They considered it a privilege to share the stage with one as beautiful as her.

A Kissing Fish

One summer afternoon, my lady and I were sitting in a boat on a lake, where the water was so calm and clear that the bottom could be seen. It seamed like we looking into a mirror when we looked over the side. Suddenly, there appeared fishes below forming a line as if they were expecting the "unexpected." Out of nowhere, a fish came swimming toward the boat so fast that it caused a small ripple in the water. It came to a sudden stop at the side of the boat. We saw it was a kissing fish, with its lips puckered. My lady fell back into my arms as the fish rose to the surface of the water. The kissing fish looked at her as if it wanted a kiss. The shocked, disdainful expression on her face could clearly be understood without words. She shouted, "What an ugly fish you are! You had better go and find your own kind!" I looked over the side of the boat, laughing as the kissing fish swam away, and shouted, "Pal, this one is mine!"

Beautiful Flower

Good morning, to my beautiful flower at the other end of this message. Hummingbirds travel so far to see the beauty of your petals as they spread apart. Bees stop by to collect your nectar to make their honey. I brought my lady by to see you because she is my best friend, love of my life, companion and wife. I will cherish, provide for and be with her forever. Your petals are so beautiful; butterflies land, flapping their wings. The stem that supports and holds up this beautiful flower is so green that it has to be noticed also. The wind from the hummingbird's wings blows across her petals, creating a magnificent movement of them. Pictures truly could not begin to capture the magnificent movement of this unique flower.

Her Morning Beauty

Oh my God, she goes through the day with very little or no make up on her face. She catches the eyes of those who see her beauty when she walks by. I stood a short distance away watching her. She moved with such fluid movements of grace and dignity that she seemed to float. She cannot help but to be noticed. When nightfall comes and she lies by my side, it is a beautiful thing to watch her as she falls asleep. When I awake next to her, I say to my Lord, "I sure do thank you for my lady's morning beauty."

Just For You

The sun refuses to shine because the clouds demand it stays hidden. There is a war going on and in a defiant way, the sun begins to show its strength. It causes the clouds to cry and sends liquid sunshine just to let you know, I have not forgotten about you. When the war is over, the sun shines to brighten your day because it wants you to know over here is someone who loves you.

Glorious Morning

How are you feeling this glorious morning? I am doing just great. Today is going to be wonderful because I know I am loved by the very best that God has given to humankind. You are a wonderful and beautiful sweetheart, one who makes me smile, laugh and glow. You are also one who knows and understands me in such a short period of time. I feel that I can walk with you onto the biggest stage to shout out and let the world know I have found my soulmate. Thank you, my lady, for bringing out the best in me.

But A Moment

If I had but a moment, I would have to say good morning my lady. If I had something to do with the rainbow, everyone would know because its beautiful colors would create a picture of you. If I had something to do with the stars, they would form a picture of your face and everyone would see it. If I had something to do with the hearts of men, they would all know that I am in love with you. I feel as if I can touch the sky because of all the joy you have brought into my life.

Hello Darling

Hello darling, how are you doing? I am trusting that my God has blessed and kept you for me. He has brought us together as one under one love, one unity and one belief. He has bound your and my heart together and has made them one. That is why we can see eye-to-eye and finish each other's thoughts. He has made us to bloom in a dark world, to glow and shine bright even when we are apart. He has made us to shine so brightly, that others always ask, "Why are you always smiling with your heads held high?" We respond back, "We have joyful hearts and peaceful minds and it is all because of God."

Vision Of My Heart

Good morning, baby. How are you? I had a vision and in that vision, there you was. Your hair is long, dark and beautiful and your face is made up. Your beauty causes my heart to skip a beat. Your lips look delicious, reminding me of red cherries, and I wish I could kiss them now to see if I am dreaming. The glow on your face causes the sun to bow, the clouds to cry liquid sunshine and the moon to rise just to see why. The stars twinkle trying to wink but you remind them you are in love with me. You say to them all, "Maybe next time; my heart belongs to the man that I love. He is the reason I am smiling so brightly. He said to me, "I love you and I cannot wait to see you."

Lifetime Valentine

Good morning my valentine. I am thinking about you. Man has been giving woman cards, candy and flowers for a long time and, for some, that is ok. However, I want to give you something that will last you always because you are my lifetime valentine. I give you and only you my heart for the rest of our lives. You are the valentine that I love all year round. Your love and beauty is enough to sustain me. The comfortable feeling I get when I hold you in my arms is enough to keep me happy in all times, good or bad, in or out, up or down, thick or thin. What I am saying is, baby, I love you with all of my heart and my heart belongs only to you.

My Diamond

I am rejoicing on this end because God has given me what I have been looking for a long time, YOU. The sun may not shine, rain may not fall and even if the wind blows in a different direction, you will still be my diamond. Never in my life have I found someone who reminds me of me. You are my diamond which has been cut, shaped, formed and shined to brighten my day. Girl, you are worth the wait because the love that flows from you keeps me feeling as if I am on the world's greatest high.

My Lady

I loved the way she looked as she entered the door. Everyone noticed there was something special about her. Her hair was stunning and her skin was glowing from the lighting reflecting upon her just right. She moved with a special grace and everyone knew that she was one of a kind. She is a woman of class, an elegant, sophisticated woman who knows what she wants. Women started to clap and the sound grew as if someone was playing drums with a soft touch. It moved across the room as men stood in respectful acknowledgment of her. She turned her head scanning the room until she found who she was looking for, me. She started toward the center of the room and made her way to the table where I was, as I arose pulling out her chair, seating her next to me. People were watching as she slowly sat down while I pushed her seat underneath her. She looked up at me with a smile on her face and with her beautiful lips uttered the word, "Thanks." I returned to my seat and someone said to me, "What a beauty you have." I graciously said, "Thank you," just before a bell rang out. "Dinner is served," cried the waiter, just as I had turned my attention back to my lady. I arose and took her napkin, unfolded it with care and laid it across her lap. She reached for me, giving me a gentle kiss. I returned to my seat, lifted my hand and cried out, "Wine for my lady!" I took her by the hand and looked into her eyes as her glass was being filled with wine. I pulled a black box from my pocket, opening it slowly; her heartbeat began to quicken. She had a short intake of breath as she realized it was a diamond necklace cut into a heart shape with engraving inside. The words flowed from her lips as she read them, "Happy Valentine Sweetheart; will you be mine?"

Rosebush Limbs

Did you hear the news? Word is going around that they are talking about you. They are saying there is a queen and everyone is looking for you. Rosebush limbs are turning green and roses cannot wait to bud. Flowers across the country cannot wait until spring to start sprouting. Birds are gathering sticks and grass to build their nests. Larva are preparing to free themselves from their silk cocoons having turned into beautiful butterflies. As for me, I have you my flower, my butterfly, my queen all year round. You are as beautiful as the rose that sits on the rosebush limbs. Thanks for being my all and all, my everything.

My Star On The Floor

She entered the room and I thought she had been crying but, as she drew near, I saw she had not. There was a sparkle in both eyes and the smile on her face showed what her heart was feeling. She moved with such class that people stepped aside. The way her eyes searched the crowd, she was asking, "Where is my king?" When she laid her eyes upon him, he hastily arose and met her halfway lifting up his hand to catch hers as the entertainer cried out, "Make way for the beautiful lady." We started across the room when someone cried out, "Play a love song for the lovely lady." When the music began to play, to our surprise, it was our favorite love song. I held her close to me while dancing; one could see we had forgotten where we were by the expressions on our faces. When the song was over, I held out my arm leading my queen off the dance floor. Ladies who watched caused quite a stir with their dates because they were not escorted off the floor. They each cried out, "Why can't you be like that?" Then my queen arose to answer the question. "He called me his rose, and that I am, because he gave me his heart and you can bet, I never intend to break it. I treat him like a king because I love him. He is my best friend and soulmate; together we are one. There is no in between when it comes to us."

Warm From Your Smile

The clouds have grown tired of being overcast and have, therefore, allowed the skies to turn blue. The sunlight is shining down upon the earth to bring you, my love, what you need to keep the lovely smile on your face. The Earth is mild and invitingly comfortable where you are. Mercury and Venus are much too hot; Mars is cold and so are the other planets. Since your heart is warm and your smile is liquid sunshine, I would rather be there with you. When I am with you, the warmth of your love embraces me like a comfortable blanket. It makes me feel warm on the coldest day of the year. Your smile brings so much joy that I cannot help but smile back knowing you will always be in my heart.

My Soul Rejoicing

Volcanoes erupt because they have heard of you; oceans flip because they want to see you. The wind blows just to ruffle your hair and trees bend over to bow in your presence. Birds fly against the wind enjoying it as if it was the first flight. However, as I stand here watching you, my soul rejoices from your beauty. All I can think is, "What a beauty; there is nothing else I would rather have than you. I love you darling, my rose, my tulip, my heart."

Rev. Leroy Wright Jr.

A Show For My Lady

A blue jay landed on a windowsill tilting its head from side to side to see through the glass. To its surprise, there sat a beautiful lady not far from the window. The blue jay started to sing an enchanting song that caught the attention of all the other birds. One by one, they all gathered around and joined in on the song. The noise grew louder and louder; the squirrels heard it and came running from all over the neighborhood. The song was so sweet that the squirrels started to dance putting on a show to get my lady's attention. People passing by stopped to watch because they had never seen anything like this before. My lady noticed what was going on and arose from her seat making her way to the window. All the birds spread their wings and lowered their heads as if taking a bow. Squirrels sat up on their hind feet, tails curling backward and front feet lifted to their mouths as if trying to shout, "Thank you." Never before had it been seen, squirrels and birds singing a song together for a beautiful lady like mine. "If animals put on a performance like this for you, my lady, think what you do to my heart when I lay these eyes of mine on a doll like you. I bow before you on one knee and kiss your hand to let you know that I love you so much more."

My Best Friend

Clara, Clara, Clara, baby, baby, baby, good morning. Thank you for being you. Thank you for being my best friend and for sharing with me the highs and lows of your past. Thank you for being my wife and for choosing me to be your husband. We stand straight and tall for what is right in this life. Thank you for listening to the God in me and the God in you. See what we both would have missed had we chosen not to listen to Him. You are beautiful and could easily have chosen someone else to spend your life with. "Thank you, Jesus, for opening my eyes and letting me see the me in her. That makes me love her that much more." Thank you, baby. I love you; I truly love you.

My World

Good morning my valentine, my lovely wife. Happy Valentine's Day, and a happy day it is. I know there is a smile on your face from the joy in your heart. Welcome to my world, a world of love, peace and happiness. My world is a world of comfort where there is a lot of intimacy. This is a world where the two us just lie there holding each other. Even though distance separates us much of the time, there is so much love between us that it can be felt even when we are apart. We cling to each other knowing that in a very short period of time distance will separate us again. Our two hearts come together as one because of the love that flows between them. On this day, the sun is going to shine because it has seen the joy in both our hearts. It may not want to go down but, because of the moon, it has to be pushed forward. The stars watch from afar but can still be seen when they wink at you. I love you, my rose. You are the smile in my heart and in my world. You are my everything.

Your Kindness

Your face is more beautiful than this day. The brightness of it reminds me of your smile. The height of the heavens reminds me of how you must feel. This world reminds me of how large your heart is when it comes to helping others. Out of all that you do, still, you are never too busy to think about little old me. Thank you for that because I am your honeybee who will always be with you. I love you, my sweet rose, for your kindness.

Comfort Of Her Voice

She calls my name with such love, asking me to come and see. As I make my way to where she is, there she stands so beautiful that the sight of her makes my heart flood with joy. I am truly grateful that God, in his own way and time, has brought us together. The sound of her voice is such a comfort to me that it sends chills through my body. I know she is very pleased with our lives. I pull her to me, giving her a short kiss, just to let her know she is the only one for me.

Knock On Her Door

I felt the need to surprise my love because she shows me how much she loves me. I knocked on her door with my hands filled with a dozen beautiful, red roses and a romantic card to match. When she opened the door, the expression on her face should have been captured to place on the cover of Ladies' Magazine of the Month. The roses caused her eyes to sparkle. "Oh, how lovely these flowers are," she said. "They are just what I was thinking of." She set them in a vase on the table in front of her sofa so they could be seen by everyone who visited her. Turning, she gave me a sweet hug and said, "Baby, I love you because you touch my heart in ways no one else could. You know what I am thinking when I do not say a word and you are able to read the expression on my face." That expression is one of open adoration and love for me. Finally, she said, "Thank you, God, for blessing me with a man who does not mind showing me just how he feels."

Cannot Wait

My heart is bleeding because, when I see the picture of you, I realize how much I truly miss you. You could not begin to imagine how much I long for your touch. My heart would be filled with such joy if you were here so I could hold you as if there was no tomorrow. Sweetheart, I cannot wait to see you because I love you deeper than the mind can imagine.

Love On Her Finger

She went into the kitchen to make breakfast for us and called me to test the smoothie she was preparing. She dipped a spoon into it and asked me, "How does it taste?" I looked into her eyes and said, "Something is missing." Taking her by the hand, I selected her pointer finger and dipped it into the smoothie. I then placed her finger, laced with the delicious concoction, into my mouth, licking it off her finger very slowly. I then told her, "Love on your finger, now that is what was missing."

Enjoying My Lady

I held my lady protectively in my arms while sitting on the couch. She was totally relaxed knowing no harm would come to her. It was so comforting holding her like this. I felt like a king in love with his queen who realizes the greatest of all his riches is her. With her by my side, I feel my reign will last forever. Looking into her eyes, I ran my fingers through her curly, dark brown hair and told her what I was feeling. I said, "Baby, I love you. You make me feel so complete that this world could be passing away and I would never leave your side. You are my fashion queen, my own supermodel who could hold her own in any fashion show. God has really blessed you with a beautiful face and glowing, honey-brown skin. Your neckline is prefect and, baby, you would make some supermodels jealous. They work so hard trying to stay in shape but you are blessed by the hand of God. People watch us when we go out on the town because they are not accustomed to seeing a man holding his wife's hand. I am proud to be seen with you and I truly love you. Understand this; every time I think of you, my heart is filled with such joy. We both love the Lord and stand for righteousness. It is He who has brought us together in His own time. He has blessed us to find one another and to share our lives together. Now that we are one, there is nothing stopping us because the hand of God is leading us."

Holding Her With Care

The falling rain has turned into snow; it is piling at the door trapping us inside. The weight of the snow on the power lines has caused them to snap. Men are working non-stop to restore the power but people inside are complaining that they are working too slowly. The temperature inside begins to drop when my baby cries, "Honey I am getting cold." I looked at her and said, "Baby, I will be right back." I went into the garage to start the generator we purchased for times like these. I returned to her side, got a warm blanket and sat on the sofa next to her. She was lying on the couch in a fetal position shivering from the cold. I gently pulled her toward me positioning her head on a small pillow I had placed on my lap. I then covered her with the warm blanket as I stroked her hair brushing it back from her face to reveal the smooth contour of her prefect jaw line. I placed my arm across her shoulder as she caught my hand locking her fingers in between mine. I began to play with her hair when she turned to face me with her beautiful smile. I looked into her eyes and sensed what she was thinking as she raised her head to give me a kiss. I placed my arms around her and held her with care like the queen she really is. I traced her delicate jaw line with my finger continuing with a feather-light touch down to the nape of her neck. I brushed my lips lightly against hers and asked if she really knew just how much I love her. Her eyes filled with tears as she whispered the words, "Baby I do know. I know that you love me because of your actions. You go above and beyond my expectations to show me how much you really love me. You call me your rose and hummingbird and then melt my heart with your smile. I cannot help but tell you I love you back because you make me happier than I have ever been. You sweep me off my feet with words that touch my inner being causing my heart to skip a beat." My mind began to wonder as she was speaking, "What have I done to deserve a queen like this?" I hugged her tighter than ever before, whispering in her ear, "Baby, I will never let you go. I love you with all of my heart. I love you more than bees love honey."

A Kiss Good Night

In my dream, my heart is melting because I am so in love with you. Yet, I feel sadness because I am not near you. When I close my eyes, I see a picture of you in my arms with your head resting on my chest. I can imagine the cool air from the ceiling fan sending a cascade of chill bumps down your arm. If I was there, I would run my warm hand along your arm chasing the chill bumps away. I can see your beautiful, brown eyes when you look up at me as I brush a loose strand of hair from your face. I gently tilt your face upward for a kiss good night and we later fall asleep in each other's arms.

Six Rose Petals

Our mother is a beautiful rose who gave dad, who is the long green stem, six beautiful children, their rose petals. Each rose petal now stands on it's own because each was taught, early in life, how to share their love with others. Therefore, each rose petal's love has overflowed onto their own offspring. I thank mom and dad for the time they spent showing each one of us how to forgive when others would not forgive us. I finally have the chance to share my love with a lady who, in return, is willing to share her love with me. She tells me, "Thank you," when I show her my love which flows like a river from deep within. I told mom and dad, "Thanks for teaching my sisters, brothers and me that no matter what, where, when or how, love overcomes all." They said, "God loves us all, in spite of what man says, and He will reward all for how we treat others."

Thinking About You

I am sitting here thinking about you. I could be on my knees holding your hand and looking into your eyes. I could be rising toward you to kiss your "oh so kissable" lips. I could be holding you so close that wind from a fan could not pass between us. I could be sitting beside you or across a table from you while having lunch with you. But since I cannot do any of these things at the moment, I can say, "I am in love with you. My heart is a rose bush with nothing but the best red roses, some that money cannot buy. These are roses that grow and flow from within… priceless."

Sight In My Mind

I want to send something special to let you know I love you. I want you to know, when I think of you, my whole world changes. You become the vision I see when I close my eyes. When I think of you and take a deep breath, I am reminded of the perfume you wear. I put my arms around you when you come to sit beside me. I can feel your body sinking deep into my arms as you tell me, "Baby, I trust you with all of my love. I trust you with my heart, knowing you care, because your love for me is true." I love you my wife, my best friend for life.

Wanting To Know

I climbed a tree but it was not high enough to see how high your love goes, so I caught an airplane. The airplane could only stay up for a short period of time so it had to come down. I took the space shuttle and landed on the moon to search for your love. The rotation of the earth and moon was too fast so I had to come back to earth. I rented a boat but it could not take me underwater so I caught a submarine to find out how deep your love goes. I could not find the end so I came back to earth to find your love here waiting for me. That is when I realized I do not have to travel all over the world looking for your love. I just looked within my heart where you planted the words, "I love you." Thank you, baby, because you let me know just how much you really love me.

Blackberry Pie

I found myself picking blackberries for my queen as she sat waiting in the car. The blackberries had grown so thick up the side of a mountain, I had lost track of time trying to fill the two large buckets I carried up. After filling both buckets, I looked down from my lofty position and realized everything below appeared very small. Something I could not identify moved off to the right at the foot of the mountain. It looked like a beautiful flower being blown by the wind. As I made my way down, drawing closer to it, I noticed it was my flower waving at me. I set one of the buckets down to wave back so she would know that I could see her. I could not wait to reach the bottom to be with my flower who was waiting for me. When I reached the bottom of the mountain, I set both buckets down quickly as she came running straight into my arms. With her arms around my neck and mine around her waist, I swung her around like she was a little girl. Afterwards, she looked up at me with her lovely, brown eyes and we found ourselves kissing as if we had been apart for a very long time. I looked at the berries in both buckets thinking I had spilled them but not one had fallen out. We started the car for our drive home and it became our chance to see one of the most beautiful sunsets known to man. The sun was just going below the mountaintop, as if it was starting to rest on its summit. She reminded me to bring our camera on our next outing because we missed our chance to record a picture-postcard moment. It was a lovely drive because there she sat next to me, the lady I love, with her head on my shoulder. We arrived home, washed the berries and made a blackberry pie. I decorated the center of the top crust with two slightly overlapping hearts shaped of dough. I wanted her to know that it symbolized our two hearts, full of love for each other and beating as one, which would last for an eternity.

Private Picnic

Early one Saturday morning, I drove to pick up my lady who was waiting for me; we were going on a private picnic. I knocked on her door and she invited me in. After picking up the basket of food she had prepared, I extended my arm and led her to my truck. We drove to a quiet, lovely place down by the lake where an oak tree stood just off in the distance. We spread a blanket and set up a small table just tall enough to lean on. We listened to soft, slow music as I rested my head on two small pillows. My lady was sitting, resting her back against my chest when she noticed two red fox squirrels sitting on a large limb watching us. We watched them as they started to play, chasing one another up and down the trees and running around them. They jumped from limp to limb and tree to tree until they were out of our sight. Suddenly, we were distracted by a noise coming from the direction of the lake; we went to see what was happening. Large mouthed bass were chasing after some smaller fishes. I got my fishing rod from my truck to show her how to catch and release them. She caught her first fish and examined it while I held it. This was her first time fishing so she was quite thrilled. I remembered what she said, during our berry-picking trip, about taking pictures of the sunset.

I wished I had brought a camera to record her exciting moment. Later, we continued our picnic, enjoying the remaining time we had together. We had a wonderful time laughing and talking as we watched the sunset. This was a day we would never forget; it was one we had all to ourselves.

A Family Gathering

I awoke to the sound of the morning doves singing. Slivers of sunlight shining through the curtains and blinds had begun to fade away. Airplanes were on the move and traffic from the freeway could be heard. Now that the airplanes had moved on and the sound of the traffic had subsided, the morning doves were still singing their songs. I listened to them sing and began to wonder what the songs were about. Were they thanking God for another day or were they sending a stress call to the others? The sounds were as if the males were singing lead and the females were responding in a higher pitch. The males were in one place and the females in another, inquiring of their offspring. The males' pitch was far deeper than the females' pitch and the females were singing with much more emotion. The males were answering back as if they were not worrying about their offspring. I knew they were having a family gathering because the sounds were growing much louder as more birds gathered. I looked out the back window and could see the family of doves already assembled. I determined that, according to their size, there were three to four generations; they were all having a wonderful feast. Some were in the tree and others were on the ground as they pecked the seeds that grew on the edge of the tree limbs. One male was sitting off to the left as if on guard duty. A gray squirrel scurried along the limbs of an oak tree in front of him, searching for acorns on the edge of the limbs. The dove watched very intensely until the squirrel left the tree. The squirrel jumped from the tree limb onto the power line, looking down as if it saw something that could be dangerous. It fled, as if spooked, seeking some much needed protection. The dove on the wire showed signs of relief and turned his attention back toward his family. The female sitting on the edge of the tree limb began to sing again as she called in more of the family. I began to think how nice it would be if humans could show this type of devotion and protection for their families when they all come together. We all could learn a valuable lesson from nature if we only knew where to look.

Cheerful Phone Call

My phone rang; it was my lady. The joyful expression in her voice filled my heart with immense pleasure. I knew that she loved me by the way she called my name. This was a call that we both enjoyed because, the previous month, I had created a short story that caused both of us to cry with laughter. It was one about her being on a date with someone of short stature. The story was filled with so many hilariously funny and exciting details that I could hardly tell it without laughing. To this day, I only have to say one particular word and she laughs until she cries.

Spot On The Beach

There is a spot on the beach that everyone knows about. It is the place where I often take my lady. This is a special spot because the sand is so bright and clean. Everyone knows it is the only place on the beach where she likes to sit. The water has its own beautiful, blue color and people love to go there to watch the sunset. You will never see any sea gulls flying around during the day when she is not there. Somehow, they always know when I am going to bring her. It is as if something is giving them a sign saying, "That beautiful lady is on the beach again." They fly overhead as if they are looking for something. They soar in one spot as she pulls out her camera phone and starts vedioing them. Some move up and down gliding on the air. Mullet fishes start to jump out of the water because they are being chased by a larger school of red fish which were feeding on them. Never before had I seen this where mullets jump out of the water fearing for their lives. Not one mullet jumps in the spot where my lady sits because they have respect for her. When the school of red fish had passed by, the mullets jumped and turned until they were back in the water. People stop by to speak to my lady and tell her how beautiful she looks. We sit there on the sand until the sun sets over the horizon giving us one of its most beautiful sunsets. The water and the sun come together as if the earth is swallowing the sun. The moonlight begins to shine, giving us light as I start to seranade my lady. Men and women come over to listen as I pour my heart out to her in a song. She is a beautiful vision as her skin glows under the moonlight. When the song is over, she says, "Thanks," to everyone as

I sit there holding her in my arms. We continue watching the moonlight shine on the water for a few hours. I then carry her home with a smile on her face, joy in her heart and another memory she will never forget.

Kissable Neck

To the woman I am in love with, I am thinking of you. I am picturing you in my mind, with your hair up, showing your kissable neck. I walk up behind you, placing my arms around your waist. You turn, looking lovingly into my eyes, then rest your head on my chest. In that fleeting moment, I feel the depth of your love as I place soft butterfly kisses on your "oh-so-kissable" neck. Holding you close, I feel your knees start to buckle. Your arms go up around my neck as your lips search for mine. When the passionate moment is over, I look into your eyes and say, "Honey, you are my world. I love you because you have fulfilled everything I have ever wanted in a woman."

That Fitted Blue Dress

The sun is shining but it is not smiling. It is trying to be bright but there are clouds blocking its view. It wants to shine to match the bright smile that is on my lady's face. The wind is blowing mildly, bringing a cool breeze. They both have heard we have a date for tonight. I called my lady to let her know I would be there to get her around seven o' clock. I asked that, if she did not mind, please wear the fitted blue dress which stopped me in my tracks. She said she would wear it if it pleased me. I picked her up at 6:55 p.m. When I saw her come through the door wearing that fitted blue dress, my heart started racing once again. We were on our way to a special event. It was a night that had been set aside for those who are in love. We drove to the place where the fireworks display was set up. There were sparklers to light the night. We were blessed to get a seat close to the river. The sparklers display began as my lady stood up. People started to clap during the fireworks display over the river below. To her surprise, a woman cried out, "That is a beautiful blue dress and you are wearing it well." My lady then replied to the woman, "Thank you. It was a request from my honey that I wear it tonight because he loves to see me in it." She took her seat next to me and said, "With all of my heart, I love you unconditionally." I replied, "Baby, you know my heart bleeds with nothing but love for you. My mind is flooded with thoughts of you constantly. My arms long to hold you. My love for you is deeper than we both will ever know and there is no end to what I would do for you. I truly appreciate and love you, darling, because you are the one who keeps me on a natural high which no one can charge me for being on." When the show was over and we started to leave, car horns were being blown and people were crying out to let her know she had stolen the spotlight in that fitted blue dress.

Just Holding Her

I found myself lying on the sofa with my lady in my arms during a quiet, peaceful moment. I had forgotten just how good she felt. Perhaps, in the past, I had taken moments like this for granted. Thinking along those lines, I clung to her tighter as if I had a need to protect her. The smell of her hair and her touch reminds me of how much I miss her when we are not together. My strong desire to rush home, just to be there when she arrives, sometimes surprises even me. Then it happened; my thoughts wandered off to the many times I have heard different women ask, "Where are all the good men?" My response to that question is, "They are out there and will find you when you are not looking for them. The big question is this, "Will you receive him when he approaches you or will you reject him?" Sometimes, men are rejected because the women they approach have been hurt in previous relationships. Please stop comparing all men to the one who disappointed you. You could be sending away the one sent by God. My lady was not looking for me, but I was looking for her. The God in her showed her the God in me, and here we lie in each other's arms, peacefully falling fast asleep.

Just Being God

This morning when I looked in the direction of the sun, while it was still behind the clouds, its rays changed the beauty of the sky. The sunlight shining against the background of the dark clouds showed the greatness of God's handiwork. The higher the sun rose, the brighter the day grew. As it began to peek over the clouds, I was reminded of what Isaiah said in chapter 52:2 (at the end of this verse), "He has no form nor comeliness and when we shall see him there is no beauty that we should desire him." If Jesus would have come in his glory, noone would have been able to look at him. His glorified stage is brighter than the sun. Noone can stare into the sunlight without becoming somewhat blind. Only God shines brighter than the sun. Then, before the sun can cross the sky, He has the power, knowledge and ability to fill the heavens with clouds and bring rain to show His strength. He's just being God. But, sweetheart, I sure do thank him for not making you so bright that I could not see your loving kindness, your awesome mind and your heart to accept the love I have for you. Thank you, sweetheart, for letting me be a part of your life. I love you, darling, because the thought of you causes my heart to shine throughout. So, my dear sweetheart, none of this would be possible if it was not for God just being God with a wonderful sense of humor.

Her Response

Observation Of Her Heart

Hello, sweetheart. You are my best friend, my soulmate, my husband and you, my love, let me know quite often that you truly love me with your whole heart.

I love you sweetheart in the deepest, sweetest, yet most passionate way imaginable and pray you can feel my love for you as deeply as I feel yours for me. You are the very best part of my world, baby. Had I known God had you two thirds of the way down toward the bottom of His basket of blessings for me all these years, I would have been like the little girl at Christmas time excitedly telling her parents, "I know you've gotten my favorite gift for me 'cause I saw him. I do not know his name yet but, oh, won't you please, please let me have him now. I promise I will take good care of him. I have waited so very long for him so, please, I am begging you to let me have him now. Life has been so empty and unfulfilling without him. You can keep all the other gifts if you just let me have that one now. Obviously, His answer was, "I love you my daughter and I know what is best for you. When I bless you with this most special gift of all time, it is to last the rest of your life. I must continue to prepare you to receive him, so you will know how to take care of him. He must know how to take care of you as well. Then, your union, once sealed by me, will withstand the test of time on this side of glory. So, be patient my child for the best is yet to come." I had no choice but to continue to wait, for my Father said to do so. Finally, when I felt He had forgotten about my special gift request, He gave me you, baby, and my heart continues to swell in joyful disbelief to this very second. My happiness is so great, it can hardly be contained. "Thank you, God, for loving me so much. You made me wait and you continued to shape and mold me to be the woman and wife that he needs in order to complete him. During my season of waiting, you were allowing him to go through things that helped him become the man and the husband I need in order to complete me. My God, my Father, what a union you have molded. We are now soulmates and, thanks to you, our love for each other will stand the test of time."

Husband And Wife

I thank God for the others who let you go. God is smiling on me like never before. You make me feel like the most beautiful, precious woman in the world. I know God has been preparing both of us all of our lives to become best friends, then husband and wife. He allowed us to go through the things that we have, tempered by life's ups and downs, to better love and appreciate each other and deepen our praise to Him. He created our prefect soulmate in each other. I love you.

Child Of His Choice

Good morning, baby. How sweet to wake up to a beautiful greeting like all those you send to me. God is, indeed, awesome. I never dreamed He had designs for my life that would place me with one of his most faithful, blessed of God, kind and loving, generous hearted and passionate children of His choice. The hand of God is upon you. I never thought, in a million years, He would find me worthy enough to bless me to share life and love with a man so highly favored by Him. I truly love you so much and it is much easier now to admit it than to hold back. Do you realize you have planted seeds of growth in various areas of my life that I am amazed about? You awakened emotions in me that I felt destined to never feel again. Thank you for seeing and knowing what I was capable of feeling, even though I did not easily allow you to get close to me. However, you handled that knowledge with gentle patience and persistence. You loved me back into trusting you enough to tear down all my protective barriers, which I had taken such care to build. Thank you, baby.

Kissing Rain

Good morning, sweetheart. You bring sunshine to my world even when the rain is kissing the earth on a day like today. If this is all a dream, it is the sweetest I have ever had and I do not want to wake up. The man who sends me these beautiful greetings and exhortations of his feelings for me really does exist. I know this for he has held me in his arms and I have felt the warmth of his embrace wash over me in a most soothing, comforting way. I have listened to the rhythmic beating of his heart next to mine thinking of it as a promise of life together.

My Heart's Desires

Good morning, honey. My, my, my, what joy you place in my spirit. What light you place in my world. If I thought I was a good person, you inspire me to be a better person. You know you are spoiling me, don't you, by waking me up each morning to words from the man who loves me? When I see you again, please pinch me so I have additional assurance you are my heart's desires wrapped in flesh and bone. I want to be certain you are not just a wishful figment of my imagination. You give me flowers, gifts and chocolates everyday through your words and the laughter you bring into my world. My love for you and my bond with you grows stronger with each passing day. I do not know if there is a ceiling or a floor to encase it. I suspect it is like infinity; it knows no boundaries. There is no containing it. There are no barriers to it. I look forward with eager anticipation for the amazing things God will unfold for us in our future together. I love you deeply and unconditionally, honey.

God's Orchestration

Baby you make me feel so loved and protected. You are there and I am here but already I feel your loving, protective presence surrounding me. "My God, my God, how magnificent, how awesome, how wonderful, Hallelujah! Hallelujah! In the mighty name of Jesus! Thank, you Lord, for blessing sinful natured little old me so richly. You have blessed me, my God, with a man after your own heart who loves, worships, adores and fears you in a most profound way. I did not find him or him me. YOU orchestrated our relationship by a divine ordering of our footsteps. YOU allowed things in our lives to take predestined twists and turns so we would end up at this moment in time. We are now reaping the benefit of your blessings found in each other. Praises for you, my Father, will continually be in my mouth, my heart and my spirit. I will send them forth with my whole heart, oh God, until they reach the heavens above and mix with praises of the heavenly hosts as I bow in humble submission and gratefulness before you. In the name of Jesus, in the mighty name of Jesus, you are Lord of my life and my personal Savior; thank you for blessing me with my soulmate and future husband. I promise, oh God, to love him fiercely, to protect his heart, to be a blessing in his life, to be a help "meet" and a helpmate, bringing joy and laughter to his life. I will join him in praising you joyfully and in the fullness of our spirits each and every day until, one glorious day, we enter into your gates when our time on this side is fulfilled. Amen! Amen! Amen!" I love you baby. The urge to praise God came over me and was so great I could not suppress it.

Romantic Message

Oh babe, you are a beautiful man with such a kind spirit. You are a shining example of how we should all be. It is truly amazing to me that you could live though all the difficulties of life and love and still be such a romantic with such an optimistic outlook and zest for life. You look forward to life with such eager anticipation that it is contagious. Thank you, baby, for that beautiful, romantic message I woke up to. I keep re-reading it with this huge smile on my face as my heart swells with love for you. Through your communications, you have shown me an equally sweet side of love. Thank you for allowing me to love you, baby, without boundaries and restraints. I promise you will never regret it. I want to bring as much joy to your world as you have brought into mine. I love you; everyday spent knowing you are in my life is a day in paradise.

Incredible Love

Good morning back to you, baby. I just finished reading some of your messages, too. They are incredible. Love opens up depths of expression people never even know they have. Baby, you are the "o" in my Fruit Loops, the raisins in my Raisin Bran and the peanut butter in my Reese's cup. You are everything good and sweet in my life. My heart flutters every time I think of you. I love starting and ending my days and nights in communication with you. During those times, I find myself thinking, "Oh how wonderful it is to be loved by you." Although distance is separating us, my heart still belongs to you.

Broken Walls

Baby, you have me feeling like I am on top of the world. I savor and embrace every emotion you bring into it. I trust and love you, so I know you will bring only that which is meaningful and beneficial to me. Before you entered my life, I was quietly existing behind many safe walls, which I had barricaded myself behind. Thank you for not taking, "No" for an answer but, instead, you gently pushed, prodded and encouraged me to live life outside the walls. The prize which waited outside those walls is so valuable, its worth cannot be tallied - wonderful you! Baby, every time I hear your voice, every time I look into your eyes, every time I see you smile, every time you hold me close, every time you kiss me it takes my breath away. I know I am the richest woman in the world because you are in my life.

In Due Season

When life deals with you harshly or unfairly, I am here to comfort you, to soothe away your frustrations, to quench your anger, to dry your tears, to make your home a peaceful oasis where love, honor, respect, joy and happiness abide. I want to be your helpmate. I will be proud to become your wife, in due season. I want you to feel as if you have a new beginning every day that you wake up with me beside you. I do not always expect you to feel on the up side of life. We all have days when we are feeling down. However, we will find out, during those times, why you are feeling that way and you will allow me to love you through it until all is right with your world again. God created me to bring true love, joy and balance to your world and to be whatever you need me to be for you. I am so happy to finally know this and fit the final puzzle piece of my life in place; I now see the full picture. Thank you for loving me. I am truly grateful that you are persistent by nature and insisted on allowing God to plant you in my life as the gift that you are. You are designed and created especially for me. I love you, baby, now and forever.

Blessed Woman

Good morning, sweetheart, "Beautiful are the feet of those who hasten to the Lord". You are beautiful and yes, you are truly my best friend, my mentor and my future husband. I am the most blessed woman in the world and I give God all the praise. Sweetheart, natural, you give me flowers, chocolates and poetry everyday through the messages you send me. It is wonderful to know that I matter to someone that much. I love you so much. You put me on a natural emotional high where I feel like a balloon floating up, up, up and I do not know if I will ever land again.

Special Kind Of Trust

Darling, I know you will never let me fall. I trust you and only you like that. In addition, I do not take your confiding in me lightly. It means the world to me that you place that kind of trust and confidence in me. Even though you share your innermost thoughts and experiences with me, you know they will stay with me and remain yours. It makes me love you even more.

Teary-Eyed

Honey, you have no idea how you make me feel. I would love to be there in your arms knowing that I am safe and protected by someone who loves me. I would never want to let go or be let go of by you. I read the first text you sent me to my co-worker and its sweetness brought her to tears. She said you should share your feelings in a book. I did not comment on that other than to say I told you the same thing. Thank you, sweetheart, for allowing your love for me to be such an inspiration in expressing your deeply personal feelings for me. They leave me teary-eyed, breathless and wanting to be with you. Once again, I love you babe.

Deep Expressions

Good morning, sweetheart. I lie here reading those beautiful messages, repeatedly, with my hand over my heart. My heart is so full of love for you that it feels like it could burst. I know some women do not receive daily written exhortations from their soulmate expressing the deeply pure and complete love he has for them. Therefore, I do not take these soul-stirring messages from you for granted. Thank you for blessing me with your love. I do not write with the depth of emotion and beauty as you do, however, I love you just as much. You have my whole heart now and forever. I have eyes only for you. I will be thinking of you and smiling all day.

Master's Hand

Good morning, sweetheart. I was lying here hating to get up because it is cold. Then, I heard the little chime from my phone, which indicates I have a text message. I read both messages and, now, I am lying here with a smile on my face and a song in my heart. It melts when I think of you. You are not the only one in love, baby. Your rose on this end blooms because of you. You keep its soil rich with an owner's tender, loving care, always letting it know it is loved and appreciated. It is then touched with morning dew from the Master's hand. This is His seal of approval to you. He is pleased with the way you have nurtured this rose back to full health and made it feel and look beautiful again. Baby, your love for me is the best medicine in the world for the neglect that ailed me. Thanks to you, I am completely whole again and madly in love with you. I am so happy that I am your only patient. You have left all others to someone else's care and now you focus your full attention on me. Thank you, Dr. Wright, for allowing me to love you back.

Uniquely Created

Thank you, baby, for all the things you do for me. You really keep me warm with your love. The security and peace in knowing how much you love me wraps around me like a warm blanket which no amount of cold can penetrate. You are my anchor in the storm and my gladiator when others try to advance against me in anger.

You are my rock in a crisis and my protector when others try to misuse me. You are the sweetest, most soothing balm in the world when my nerves are frayed. Darling, you are my comforter, my hero, my everything. God uniquely created YOU just for me and He created ME for you. He allowed our hearts to be tested and branded in the fires of our past relationships to strengthen us for the depth of love, commitment and appreciation we feel for each other now. How sweet it is to be loved by you; how sweet it is to be in love with you. Thank you, baby, for everything you are to me.

Rare Jewel

Good morning, sweetheart. You always know exactly what I need and when I need it. I have read and re-read these beautiful outpourings of your heart several times since awakening. I have no doubt that you have removed all barriers and all defenses. You have left your heart fully open, raw and vulnerable to me. Rest assured, however, because of my deep, pure love for you, I will guard your heart as if it was my own. I will never betray you or willfully hurt you. You are the best of everything good in my life. God has truly blessed us with something rare and magical. This special love we share with each other is one we do not take lightly. You are my world, one I dreamed of but did not think really existed. You are also a precious jewel and I share the reign of queen in your life with you as king in mine. Together, we are nurturing and enjoying a dynasty of true love. No one but God can ever separate us. I love you so much. Thanks for being the man that you are and for choosing me to love.

Totally Convinced

Oh my, you have left me speechless. I am all choked up. I feel so much love for you. You saved me by throwing me a life raft of love to keep me from drowning in a self-made sea of nothingness, full of colorless days and nights. What began as a comfort zone had become my prison. No one but you could see me for who and what I was in this prison. You pulled me through the bars of it gently with love, kindness and reassurance. Your freeing me has shown me what I have been missing by not allowing the right man to love me. God created us for each other from the very beginning. I know that now. I am totally convinced of it. The many things we have in common are unveiled more and more in each deep conversation we have. I cannot thank you enough, baby, for loving me deeply and purely. In return, I give you my whole heart and the best of everything within me. I listen to your wise counsel and I thank God for you. He has blessed me with a true helpmate. You advise me on matters that weigh heavily on my heart and you bring me joy in so many other ways. I am finally truly happy because of you. You did this for me and not only do I love you fiercely, but I thank you. Yes, I do.

Deeply Affected

Good morning, darling. Thank you for those beautiful words you awakened me to. Only you can write such words that affect me so deeply. I can feel your love for me through your words as I open my heart to receive them. I do not have the gift of poetry and prose but I can tell you that I love you deeply, seriously and committedly. My heart belongs only to you. Sweetheart, I know I can trust you to realize that I really do mean it. I love you.

Heartfelt

Good morning, baby. I was lying here listening to the rain outside wishing you were here. I know that if you were, my world would be perfect. Then a ping from my phone alerted me that my best friend, the wonderful man in my life, had sent me a message from his heart. When I read it, it was as if you were before me on one knee with your right hand placed over your heart. You were giving me all truth, all honest raw emotion of a very private moment between you and God. This was during a very difficult time in your life when you, His child, were crying out for Him to come see about you. He needed to make everything alright that you had gone through up to that point in your life. Actually, He knew when He made you those very pleas would reach him. He had been preparing me all of my life to be His answer to your prayers. I knew I was made to love, honor, praise, worship, obey and adore Him. Truly, I do, but I was at a point in my life where I questioned Him as to what the other earthly purpose for my life was. I felt something was off balance somehow but could not define what that could possibly be; my mind was telling me I should be content. Oh, but when He moved in what seems now like the blink of an eye, He ordered your steps and actions to shake the cage I was locked in. The doors swung open freeing me to be embraced in your heart and your arms. In that moment, you knew He had answered your very specific prayers. I knew He had answered the utterances of my spirit at a time when I did not know what to pray for. I thank God for being who He is and for orchestrating our love for each other. I love you, baby, in the deepest most profound way imaginable. I will be by your side always.

Beautiful Greeting

Good morning, my heart. I woke up to these beautiful greetings from you that make me feel as if I awakened in your loving presence. Hmmm, I love you baby. Your love keeps taking me higher and higher and I do not want to ever land. I truly wish you were here to enjoy this moment with me. Have a blessed day!

Patiently Waiting

Good morning to you, too, sweetheart. I feel that God will someday bring us together as husband and wife. While we are apart, I feel God still wants us to learn something of great value. We will figure it out as we go. Like Daniel in the lion's den, we must remain strong, have faith, and encourage each other. Here is a quote I heard and wrote in the front of my bible about Daniel's experience. "If like Daniel, you are waiting in a den of helplessness, spend the time as he did trusting God. Nurture the wait with trust and deliverance will come." I trust God knows our hearts and how badly we want to be together. When the right season comes (after we both have been fine-tuned to His satisfaction), He will grant us our heart's desire. We will be a loving, God fearing, husband and wife couple under one roof. I love what God had done in our lives in bringing us together.

Growing Together

Hi, darling, I can feel your love for me in your words and they bring me comfort, joy, reassurance and sheer happiness. Your words set my heart aflutter. After God, we are the best medicine in the world for each other. You are my daily dose of wonderful; my heart does not have to be pried open to receive you and all that you bring into my world. In the days and years ahead, as you grow, I want to grow with you. As you learn, I want to learn with you. As you live and love, I want to live and love with you and be right by your side in rough waters and calm seas. Come what may, I will never waver or leave your side. I want to feel like your second skin, one you don't mind wearing. I want to help bring our love for each other to a new level. To God be the glory for allowing me to fulfill my other purpose, which is being your biggest fan, your best friend and wife. Thank you, baby, for giving me something no other woman has, your whole heart and a love like no other.

Special Bond

Good morning, handsome. I love spending time with you whenever possible. I, for example, love the bonding experience that we share on date nights. Your holding my hand at the movies makes me feel especially close to you. I hope today is a perfect day for you with everything falling into place exactly as you wish. I will keep smiling as I think of you and how much I love you.

Excited Schoolgirl

Good morning, honey. I am always excited to hear from you and it is an especially treasured gift when I see you. I am like a giddy schoolgirl before your arrival. During your last visit, I thought that, of all the places we talked about visiting, Jamaica sounded like the most exciting. By the way, I love the way you talk seriously to me about our future and then, out of nowhere, you fill me with laughter from deep within. Thank you for making me the happiest woman in the world.

My Jewel

Good morning, baby. Yes, the Lord is good. It is so reassuring to know of and feel his love for us and of how He constantly intercedes for us to God, our Father. Grace, what a daily blessing He gives us. I was reading some of the loving, past messages you sent me when I received this morning's encouraging message. You always know when I need to be encouraged. I am so grateful to God for guiding your heart toward mine. What a jewel you are to me. I am the wealthiest woman in the world for I have you. I will always love you, sweetheart. Always.

Lifetime Promise

Hi, sweetheart. I want you to know that you are my sunrise at the beginning of each day and sunset at the end. My heart resides in yours always. I live to hear your voice, know your thoughts and imagine a lifetime with you of love and purpose. God has again fulfilled the promise He gave me all those many years ago in Psalm 24:14. Sweetheart, I love Him and will serve Him until the day I leave this place and beyond, but while here, will count every second with you a joyful blessing for you are that promise.

Positive Attitude

Good morning my husband, my love, my soulmate, my very best friend, my mentor and teacher. You have been sculpted by God just for me. Oh, how wonderful it is, baby, to bask in the sunshine, security and comfort of your love. You totally complete me in a way no one has ever done. I love everything about you. You have a heart and a mind for God first and then family which includes me. We are so much alike. I love the similarities, your sense of humor and quirkiness, your passion for your beliefs in the things you undertake to do. I also love your positive attitude and your resolve to stay the course, trusting God in the face of life's trials and tribulations. You are my tall, refreshing drink of water. Spending quality time with you is like quenching my thirst at the well of life. You are so darned handsome, baby, that my thoughts of you take my breath away. I thank others for letting you go. They threw you, their diamond, away and I found you. Now you are mine, all mine and unlike the others before me, I am never letting you go. I love you with my whole heart. You are everything I ever dreamed of in a soulmate (my total package.) Now, I am wealthy beyond measure because I have you by my side. Thank you, baby, for being the wonderful man you are and for choosing me to love. I promise to love, honor, respect and obey you now and always as my husband for life.

To everyone of you who has read my book and gained a deeper understanding of how to better your relationships, "Thank you." I hope you were able to understand the emotions that were expressed in these writings. I pray that it helped you enough to want to share the book with your friends to help better their relationships. My prayers are that it also helps strengthen your own relationship. I know that not every woman or man will be able to understand and accept some of the heartfelt thoughts and emotions that I have shared with my wife in this book. Negative attitudes will cause some to never hear the words, "I love you." If those words were said, they would not be from the heart but instead would be words that just rolled off a loose tongue. No man or woman with a positive attitude will be content with someone with those other types of negative emotions. Negative attitudes from others will cause a God-fearing man or God-fearing woman to withdraw and hold his or her feelings within. Remember, pride leads to destruction. If you have some of these traits, think about getting them under control. The words, "I love you," will not come from the heart, if spoken by someone with a hellraising, uncontrollable tongue. Remember, the Bible states, "Blessed are the peacemakers: for they shall be called the children of God." Men and women, if you want to be treated like a king or queen learn how to treat one another with love and respect. Remember she was your queen and he was your king at the beginning of your relationship.

Printed in the United States
By Bookmasters